7 DAYS BEHIND THE VEIL

THRONE ROOM MEDITATIONS

John Paul Jackson

Streams Publishing House

7 Days Behind the Veil: Throne Room Meditations by John Paul Jackson

Copyright © 2008 by John Paul Jackson
All rights reserved. Third edition.

No part of this book may be reproduced without written permission from the publisher.

Published by Streams Publishing House
www.streamsministries.com
1.888.441.8080

Unless otherwise noted, Scripture quotations are taken from the New King James Version, Copyright 1979, 1980, 1982 by Thomas Nelson, Inc., Publishers. Used by permission.

This book incorporates content from John Paul Jackson's audio teaching *Mystery of Movement* (Copyright © 2006 John Paul Jackson, Streams Ministries International) and other sources.

Editor: Lauren Stinton
Editorial Assistant: Leslie Herrier
Cover and interior design by Jonathan Bohy

ISBN: 1584831235
Library of Congress Control Number: 2006931931
Printed in the United States of America.

FOR MORE INFORMATION
USA: www.streamsministries.com
Canada: www.streamscanada.com
1.888.441.8080

DEDICATION

*To seekers of God
who are not content with
the outer courts.
To men and women
who are beside themselves
in love with God.*

*"Thou hast made us for thyself,
O Lord, and our hearts are restless
until they find their rest in thee."*
— St. Augustine —

Acknowledgments

*N*othing I do is ever separate from my wife, Diane; this book is no exception. Her intimacy draws me closer to God, and her faithful support carries me through.

I am grateful to the Publishing staff who helped bring this book to life: Lauren Stinton, who oversaw the writing and art development; Leslie Herrier, who served as editorial assistant; and Jonathan Bohy, whose creative talents fashioned this book into the work of art it is.

Many thanks also to proofreaders Mary Ballotte, Susan Stinton, Joni Cooper, and Judy Sargent, who took time out of their schedules to help perfect the manuscript.

And as always, the rest of my staff deserves recognition for the effort and support they've shown Diane and me, not just during the production of this book but continually.

INTRODUCTION

How do you describe a spiritual experience with human words? It is like trying to speak an entirely different language, one that only you know. For example, if the thought comes to you in English, it won't be *exactly* the same thought when it's translated into Chinese. Even if the translation were given by the best interpreter in the world, no one could possibly know what was going through your head when you said it. Except for God, no one heard your thoughts or saw the pictures in your mind. And so it is with a spiritual experience expressed with human words. No matter what one says, words alone will not be able to say it all.

When an individual visits God's throne room, no matter how brief that visit may seem, that person is changed. At some level, his or her spiritual makeup and even physical cellular structure have been altered. When I say, "You are never the same again," it is not meant to be a cliché. It is literal—it is a very, very real change that happens.

Some years ago, I had a spiritual encounter that has affected every subsequent moment of my life. It has made me realize how desperately we need to have a greater and grander view of eternity—one that dramatically reworks the small view we have from earth. In order to implement the fullness of God into our daily lives, our view of eternity and spiritual life must be so much larger than our temporal existence here. We are not human beings having a temporary spiritual experience; we are spiritual beings having a temporary human experience. We could never describe the whole of eternity, its beginning or ending, for God has no beginning. He has no ending. All was created by the sound of His voice or with His own hands. He has always simply *been*, stretching on and on before us, and on and on after us. He will always *be*.

Just that one thought will play with your mind if you spend much time on it. This is another reason it is hard to explain spiritual things—because most of us simply do not have the mental framework for them. Logic can be a cruel master.

Timeless is a descriptor we assign to a special movie or book that really speaks to us; we can't comprehend what it means with God. Timelessness is far superior to this temporal realm we live in.

Simply put, we need to let go of every small concept we have gripped in the past and reach for what is truly real. This metamorphosis is one of the first spiritual shifts that happens when you visit the Father's throne room—you realize very quickly what is important in life and what is not. In the blink of an eye, priorities are laid out in proper order. Your life takes on new meaning, new depth, because you cannot *not* be changed when standing before the throne of the most powerful, most dangerous, most attractive Being in, or out of, the universe. In one nanosecond, everything about you is affected by Him. Everything is changed, both the physical and the nonphysical — the spiritual quickly becomes more tangible, more consuming, and more real than the physical ever could be. This is why it is extremely important to fully grasp Proverbs 3:5: "Trust in the LORD with all your heart, and lean not on your own understanding." We can understand God only with God's mind. Nothing else is big enough.

Eternity is timeless and it is the realm God lives in — the one He wants us to live in with Him, even here on earth. It is a realm that reaches beyond our imagination, beyond our capability to understand, and beyond our mental, time-constrained reasoning. Entering God's realm teaches us, stretches us, and prepares us in ways we never thought possible, for it is unimaginable.

It is my hope that in reading this book, you will touch something you've only dreamed about, and at that moment of touch, you will realize that your dreams were far too small. Intimacy with God begins in His throne room.

— *John Paul Jackson*

CONTENTS

DAY ONE .... *Standing Before the Throne* 13
DAY TWO ...... *To Dwell Among Men* 25
DAY THREE ..... *Creation Declares His Glory* 35
DAY FOUR ...... *On Earth As It Is in Heaven* 47
DAY FIVE .... *Worship and Creativity* 59
DAY SIX .... *Love's Effect on Personal Identity* 71
DAY SEVEN ..... *Worship: An Instinct* 83

Day One

*"By His Spirit He adorned the heavens;
His hand pierced the fleeing serpent.
Indeed these are the mere edges of His ways,
And how small a whisper we hear of Him!
But the thunder of His power who can understand?"*

— JOB 26:13–14 —

JOHN PAUL JACKSON

STANDING BEFORE THE THRONE

Nothing can truly prepare you for standing before the throne of God. For the first time in your life, nothing holds Him at a distance. There are no boundaries; there are no safe zones. His power is all-consuming, and each wave convinces you more and more of two things: You are dead should the thought ever cross His mind... and *nothing could ever be like Him*.

Nothing can prepare us for this sort of experience—this sort of *realization*. Every inch of our body is incredibly aware of and terrified by His power. Every inch of our soul burns at His proximity. He is more than we could think possible. Being in the throne room is one of the most glorious, most frightening experiences we could ever have.

Standing there, I thought I was going to die. I was not a brave man before Him. Touched by His fervent, burning power, I knew that if He were to even *think* a single, random thought, it would be done. *Just like that.* I prayed that random thought would not be about me.

At the same time, I was aware that God knows every detail about every single thing in existence—even those things that are not yet. There is nothing outside His knowledge. He knows what it is, where it is, why it is, and what will happen to it before the end. He knows its past, present, and future. He knows every cell in every physical and nonphysical body—every subatomic particle. He knows every piece of sand in every crystal in every stone in every mountain. He knows every *thought* of every creature, all at the same time. Nothing is beyond Him. Nothing is outside of Him.

Beyond the Mind

In one instant—just one encounter—we are changed forever, even if His touch seemed small or insignificant to us at the time. Even if we forget seemingly brief, daily encounters, our spirit will always remember and continually attempt to pull our mind, will, and emotions back toward Him, to bring us once again into the flame of His presence. We are changed forever by each encounter. We are truly regenerated.

That is what His presence does to a person. Without even trying, just because He is who He is, He steps beyond everything we have ever thought of or tried to comprehend. He flows beyond everything we could ever hope for. He goes beyond our wildest dreams, and being a prophetic people, we know what it is like to dream *wild*. He is more than we could imagine, more than we could ever touch or know fully, even if we had a million years and each year lasted a million years. We could never reach the end of Him, and we will never cease to be amazed.

Yet, in the midst of all this glory, it is *His* pleasure to touch *us*. All this power, all this truth and fragrance and passion, everything He is... and it is His pleasure, His desire, to spend His time with us. We are the focal point of His heart.

Dazzled by the Love of Your Life

When we have a true God experience, our tiny view of Him bends. Depending on the level of the encounter, sometimes it completely shatters.

To compare a very human experience with a divine encounter, it is like being on an airplane and looking down toward the ground on a cloudy day. We see *nothing* but a white-gray mass. For some, studying the clouds is enough; it can take years to learn everything known about them and many more years to make our own discoveries.

But one of the awesome, mind-twisting things about God is this: Even when the clouds part, what we see is still just a glimpse. No matter how glorious, how huge, how amazing, how deep, how intricate and how impossibly beautiful it is, it is still *only a glimpse* of Him.

It is here, in the throne room's holy atmosphere, that we face the grandeur of the Creator and the Source of all that exists, visible and invisible. It is here we understand what Job was saying:

> *"I have uttered what I did not understand,*
> *Things too wonderful for me, which I did not know…*
>
> *"I have heard of You by the hearing of the ear,*
> *But now my eye sees You.*
> *Therefore I abhor myself,*
> *And repent in dust and ashes."*
>
> — JOB 42:3, 5–6 —

JOHN PAUL JACKSON

Selah Moments

Selah *is a pause, a reflection.*
The following thoughts are meant to be read
slowly, meditatively, while listening to
the heartbeat and breath
of God.

*Y*ou were created to live, breathe, and
pull your being from the heart of God.

❖

*E*verything He's done, He's done to
touch your heart.

❖

*N*othing is outside of Him.

In the midst of His unfathomable glory, power, and majesty, it is His pleasure to spend time with *you*.

❖

All He is, is available to you as His presence expands within you. All it takes is getting closer.

Day Two

Then the LORD spoke to Moses, saying: "Speak to the children of Israel, that they bring Me an offering. From everyone who gives it willingly with his heart you shall take My offering. And this is the offering which you shall take from them: gold, silver, and bronze; blue, purple, and scarlet thread, fine linen, and goats' hair; ram skins dyed red, badger skins, and acacia wood; oil for the light, and spices for the anointing oil and for the sweet incense; onyx stones, and stones to be set in the ephod and in the breastplate. And let them make Me a sanctuary, that I may dwell among them."

— EXODUS 25:1–8 —

To Dwell Among Men

The Israelites constructed the tabernacle so that the desire of God's heart would be fulfilled—that He would live among them.

Just that one sentence reveals books and books and infinite marvels and worlds of wonderings about our Father. He desires to dwell among us. Can you feel the spiritual intensity of that statement? Could you ever wrap our mind around what that truly means? It is unimaginable. It is incomprehensible.

Everything He is, everything He has touched, the worlds He has hung in place, the stars that glimmer in His eyes... All of this He has done. All of this He has spun from His fingertips—He is the incalculable artist. Nothing exists without Him. Nothing breathes without His breath (Psalm 104:29). And above all of this—He desires to dwell *here*, among us.

Whether we feel like it's true or not, we are the focal point of His heart.

He desires to dwell with us, to make His resting place in our being. He does this by making us holy vessels that mirror the holiness found in His throne room. Why was Moses to build the tabernacle *exactly* as God had shown him on the mountain? Because when we describe the tabernacle, we are describing the place where God lives—His throne room. Both places have similar furnishings, and both tell us about God.

When we are practicing holiness, we are practicing godliness, and in so doing we allow God to come and make His dwelling among and within us. There is nothing holy that does not radiate or flow from Him.

Reaching for the Holy

The reason all Heaven keeps repeating, "Holy, holy, holy," is not because that's just what they do up there, strumming along with their little golden harps. "Holy!" is a witness to what God has just done.

Every time God acts, the act is holy, and so the angels and every other heavenly creature bear witness to that holy act and cry out, "Holy!"

This cry has strata of *thickness*, because He does billions of acts every second, so there are billions of "Holy!" every second, layers upon layers of them. Yet, in the midst of all the noise, echoed by thunderings and lightnings and voices from the throne, every single voice and every single sound is distinct from every other. None of them blend together. They are each totally distinct and separate. On earth, sound isn't capable of doing that, but in Heaven, sound is *real* and much more tangible. You can feel it on your skin and sliding through your spirit—it carries weight. It has substance.

HOLY
HOLY HOLY HOLY
HOLY HOLY HOLY

This is why we worship. This is why we endeavor to be like Him. This is why we pursue Him. This is why we exist! Because Holiness desires to make His dwelling *here!* And wherever He dwells, there is union between Heaven and earth, and life takes on meaning and importance. Here we find life and breath that could *never*—in any sense of the word—be found elsewhere.

Connecting with God

Very simply, worship is connecting with God. He gave us tangible realities in His Word of what worship looks like in Heaven. He did this so that something He greatly desires could take place: We could be *connected* with Him.

He could dwell among us. Two hearts could be one. By His breath we could breathe. By His body we could live. By His existence, we could exist, so wrapped up in Him, so much in love that nothing could exist outside Him—not because He is merely consumed with having our attention, but because that is how it is when you're truly, exquisitely in love with someone. He wants us to fall in love with Him, because He is in love with us. It's that simple, and it's that profound.

Rest in His Love

Just as it is in relationships between men and women, you cannot force yourself to feel something that just isn't there. It is hard for human beings in a fallen world to comprehend the Father's heart—the true-blue, romantic, passionate, fatherly, brotherly, motherly love of God. Even though He aches to hold us, He completely respects us in all regards, including our walls.

This next statement flies in the face of traditional Christian teaching, but...we can have boundaries with God. He is not upset or angry if we cannot let Him any closer than our ten-foot-thick wall. He is okay with waiting.

He wants what is real from us. He doesn't want lip service. He is willing to wait for as long as it takes in order to capture our heart. If all we can give Him right now is a furtive, frightened glance above the wall, then He'll take that glance and patiently wait for the rest. If all we can give Him is a mere *sliver* of our true self, He'll take that piece, no matter its size...and patiently, lovingly wait for the rest.

Our walls don't send Him on a pity party. Our wrong choices don't scare Him away. Whatever we're going through right now, He knows. He understands it even more than we do, so we can't think that what we're dealing with might make Him angry at us. He already knows it; He is simply waiting for us to admit it. You see, it is in the admitting that it loses its power over us.

Don't be afraid of making mistakes. Don't worry about runaway emotions. Don't worry about the things that scare you in the deepest parts of your soul—like rejection, like condemnation. Don't be afraid of God. There is nothing in Him to condemn us. He knows, and He loves, and He fights for us more than we could imagine.

As we rest in Him, He Himself will lead us along the bridal path. After all, He is the only One who knows the way.

Selah Moments

The desire of God's heart is to dwell
with and within each of us.

❖

*N*othing breathes without His breath.

❖

*B*e prepared for God to speak to you
everywhere and anywhere.

❖

*A*s we rest in Him, He Himself will
lead us down the bridal path.

❖

*H*e waits for you.

Day Three

Immediately I was in the Spirit; and behold, a throne set in heaven, and One sat on the throne. And He who sat there was like a jasper and a sardius stone in appearance; and there was a rainbow around the throne, in appearance like an emerald. Around the throne were twenty-four thrones, and on the thrones I saw twenty-four elders sitting, clothed in white robes; and they had crowns of gold on their heads. And from the throne proceeded lightnings, thunderings, and voices. Seven lamps of fire were burning before the throne, which are the seven Spirits of God.

— REVELATION 4:2–5 —

CREATION DECLARES HIS GLORY

All throughout Scripture, we find God moving and revealing Himself. He wants to be known by us—and not just known but *touched*. He wants us to dare to put our hand into the flame of His presence. Everything He created, He created with *purpose*, a purpose that is better and more wonderful than what is humanly imaginable, even if we've spent years and years studying Him and all the possibilities.

Every single created particle, no matter how small, has purpose. It has specific reasons why it exists—profound destiny. There are no accidents in creation. God didn't sit up in Heaven and think, *Well, I'm going to create this six-winged being. I have no clue what I'm going to use it for, but I'm going to call it a seraphim. And then, just to confuse the matter, I'm going to create a four-winged creature and call that a cherubim. And just to confuse things even more, I'm going to make angels and hosts and not tell anyone much about the difference between the two — even though I know there's a big difference.*

In Heaven, as in all of creation, everything has a purpose and everything reveals *God*. The story is masterfully written, and each detail, even the ones that seem insignificant, plays a part in leading the reader to the climax.

God's fingerprints are on every element, His signature on every forehead. There are no "just becauses" with God, but clearly, that doesn't mean we can explain everything. For instance, when the apostle John writes that lightnings, thunderings, and voices come from the throne, every preconceived idea we might have about Heaven being silent is destroyed—thunderously. *Voices* come from the throne? How can there be voices when there is only One who sits there? So many things are still a mystery! Just as God intends them to be.

The Essence of Mystery

Mystery is one of the greatest lures of romance and intimacy. Its magnetism draws us, woos us, even propels us to find what we have yet to experience, to find what our heart knows is there. We can sense it. Our logic argues against it, but the mystery becomes so much our desire that in the end, we pursue it with everything we have, unmindful of the cost. We fall deeply, madly in love.

Heaven and Our View of God

Standing in the throne room is like standing in the middle of an atom. The throne is the nucleus, and protons, electrons, and other subatomic particles are whizzing past all the time. There are angels and other heavenly beings, many of which are completely beyond our current understanding. It would mentally pull us apart if we tried to comprehend them!

We tend to think of Heaven as being graveyard silent, with the angels tiptoeing across golden floors and crystal seas, whispering, "Shhh! Don't disturb God!" But this is not the case—at all. Heaven is a *noisy* place.

One of the saddest verses in Scripture is Revelation 8:1: "When He opened the seventh seal, there was silence in heaven for about half an hour." Why? Because it means that God was not doing His holy acts. He had turned man over to his own devices.

How we view Heaven greatly affects how we view God. If we think it's a dull and boring place, what does that say about God? If we think this life on earth would be much more exciting than spending an eternity "up there," then what do you suppose that does to our level of intimacy with the God who wants us to be with Him every moment of every day? Is it any wonder that so few experience the deeper levels of intimacy?

However, if we can come to the place where we realize that Heaven is so much more than the Church has traditionally thought, it will change our view of the One who lives there. *He* is so much more than we have traditionally thought.

The Whole Earth Declares His Glory

The arrangement of the throne room tells us something about God. The angels tell us something about God—

how they are shaped, how they are dressed, everything they do, the motions they make—everything tells us something about God. Read His Word with that in mind. Go to the grocery store with that in mind; you will be surprised at what He shows you about Himself in the middle of the soup aisle.

We are to live our life with the understanding that God is writing a story, and every detail plays a significant part.

This constant looking is partially what Jesus meant when He said, "If you seek, you will find" (Matthew 7:7). If we look for Him, He *will* be found. And so we discover in the seeking that what we focus on we make room for.

Selah Moments

Each of us is the focal point of His heart.

❖

If our worship doesn't involve the heart, it doesn't involve anything.

❖

What we focus on we make room for. Where is our focus—have we felt Him lately?

❖

God's fingerprints are on every element; everything, in some way or form, declares His glory.

❖

Your view of Heaven reveals your view of God.

Your view of God reveals how much
you will allow Him to do for you.

❖

Your view of God reveals the limits
you place on His power.

7 Days Behind the Veil

Day Four

"This people I have formed for Myself;
They shall declare My praise."

— Isaiah 43:21 —

Grace to you and peace from Him who is and who was and who is to come, and from the seven Spirits who are before His throne, and from Jesus Christ, the faithful witness, the firstborn from the dead, and the ruler over the kings of the earth.

To Him who loved us and washed us from our sins in His own blood, and has made us kings and priests to His God and Father; to Him be glory and dominion forever and ever. Amen.

— Revelation 1:4–6 —

On Earth As It Is in Heaven

*W*e were created to bring God glory. In other words, the purpose of our lives is for God's will to be done in them. His purpose becomes our purpose.

For some, this can be a scary statement, because we have a tendency to view God and His seemingly abstract will through the blinders of fear that the enemy has nailed up before us. We think, *If I truly let Him be Lord of my life, it's going to be boring. I'm not going to get anything I want! He's going to make me do all these dying-to-self things I don't want to do. My life will be over.* But His intent is not to make us as little and humble as possible, to squeeze us until our ego bleeds out. In fact, the point of dying to self is not to die to self. It is to be closer to Him, to be with Him, to be like Him, and to remove from our life everything that is not reflective of Him. Dying to self equals intimacy and divine romance. *He* is the point, and His intent... is us.

Love Before Anything Else

When friction comes, it usually comes because we so often resist Him. But our destiny is *Him* and Him alone; everything else is a side issue. Making disciples, preaching to presidents and kings, evangelizing thousands—whatever God has called each of us to do, He has called us to intimacy with Him first. He does not want us to pursue ministry before pursuing Him. He does not want us to try to perfect our character or to seek to be a "good Christian" before pursuing Him. It won't happen. Being a mature Christian who knows how to handle life is not the point. Relationship with God is the point. Everything else flows out from this one place. If it doesn't involve the heart, it doesn't involve anything.

How close we come to His heart, or how far we

stay away, is entirely up to us. He isn't the one holding us back. He is more anxious for us to know Him than we are—so much so, He sent His only begotten Son to reconcile us to Him.

As It Is in Heaven

Because intimacy is the focus of Heaven, one of the greatest prayers we could ever pray is this: "Your will be done on earth *as it is in heaven*" (Matthew 6, emphasis mine). Jesus taught His disciples to pray like this because He does only what He sees His Father doing (John 5:19)—what He sees Him doing in Heaven. We cannot see this without intimacy; our soul is too beguiling. Without intimacy, we will always think our will is God's will, rather than His will being ours.

We are comprised of the dust of this earth. With intricate care and affection, God formed us and fashioned us from very humble beginnings. "For dust you are," God told Adam in Genesis 3, "and to dust you shall return." God took the dust of the earth, formed it into a man, breathed into his nostrils, and man became *a living spirit*. The universe changed in that one moment.

Intimacy with man began in one breath, when His breath became ours.

And so the prayer "Your Kingdom come; Your will be done on earth" literally begins *in* you, begins in me, every day because we came from that earth. This Kingdom that lies within us needs to grow, needs to mature, needs to consume us, and eventually needs to reach out beyond us to touch other people. It cannot just live and grow inside us; it has to reach out beyond us, so that when we walk down the hallway, we touch people with the presence of God that radiates from within us. The power of God, no matter how small the magnitude, affects everything it touches the way a raging fire affects candle wax—the exterior melts away, and God becomes all in all.

Out of the Box

Jesus taught us to pray the Lord's Prayer because Heaven is reality, not earth. This is a hard-to-grasp, completely foreign concept, but what we see here on earth, all around us, is merely a shadow of reality, not reality itself (1 Corinthians 13:12). The temporal is always inferior to the eternal. So in order to touch the heart of God, we must learn to mirror on earth the activity of Heaven. Worship has everything to do with the mystery of eternity and the world beyond—all that He created.

Selah Moments

Our responsibility is to respond to the Lover's touch.

❖

Worship is an instinct.

❖

Our will is often not the same as God's will.

❖

Intimacy allows slivers of God's attributes to be passed on to us. The nearer we get to Him, the easier it is to absorb who He is.

❖

Spiritual gifts are a by-product of intimacy.

The point of dying to self is not to die to self; it is to be closer to Him.

❖

In order to touch the heart of God, we must learn to mirror on earth the activity of Heaven.

❖

Mystery is one of the greatest secrets of romance and intimacy—and God is full of mystery.

DAY FIVE

"Where were you when I laid the foundations
of the earth?
Tell Me, if you have understanding.
Who determined its measurements?
Surely you know!

Or who stretched the line upon it?
To what were its foundations fastened?
Or who laid its cornerstone,
When the morning stars sang together,
And all the sons of God shouted for joy?"

— JOB 38:4–7 —

WORSHIP AND CREATIVITY

*C*reativity speaks something from nothing. Because it involves dependency on the Spirit, the act of creating, in all its varying forms, can be worship at a level currently beyond human comprehension. Even if you never actually finish writing the poem, sculpting the piece, or painting the canvas, the boundaries between the human and the celestial have been crossed with a single line; for just a moment, all dimensions of spirit and life converge.

Dependency on the Spirit of God not only requires trust but *is* trust. True creativity is solely dependent on the One we could never create or dream up, and unless the Uncreated One reaches down from Heaven and injects revelation into us, nothing will be formed. The painting will not appear on the canvas. The haiku will not emerge from the end of our pen. Every drop of our creative ability comes from Him.

Creativity in the Throne Room

Having been in God's throne room, I have seen creativity in its finest form—creativity that embodies true, complete, *full* worship. I love artistic things. I love colors, textures, densities. I love all these things because I saw them there. The place where He dwells is moving, living, breathing creativity.

Around Him was light—light of different densities, hues, and colors. There were rings of light and layers of light, each with a different thickness, a different texture. Just as fabric has varying textures, the light He cloaks Himself in had varying textures. It went beyond everything the earth-bound mind could comprehend. It was stunning, penetrating, and transforming.

Revelation: The Birth of Creativity

All creative elements, whether art, drama, music, sculpting, poetry, or whatever else, are born from the same seed—revelation. You can't write a song without it. You can't write poetry without it. You can't design a building, write a book, or sculpt even the smallest thing without it. You can't do anything without revelation! Revelation births creativity.

Revelation (a direct encounter with the Spirit of God) allows us to take that which does not exist and put it into a form that does exist, and in this way, things that are not become things that are (Romans 4:17). So pictures and thoughts will come to our mind. They combine with dreams and visions to form some level of spontaneous outpouring that takes shape in a sculpture, chord progression, musical score, dramatic act or play, book, poem, or any other form of artistic expression. All of this is worship, because we acknowledge it came from someone far greater than ourselves. To the believer, it is the worship of God. To the nonbeliever, it becomes worship of a dark form.

Worshipping God Through Creativity

All creative people recognize that some mysterious force

greater than themselves has breathed, and from that breath, what lies before them has materialized. Something "magical" has happened. The same Holy Spirit who hovered over the face of the waters of the formless earth—and formed it—is hovering over us. In that hovering, we and that which proceeds from us are formed. Our creation rises from deep within us to take a tangible form, and we see it before it exists. As we experiment in creativity, and as the Spirit of God comes upon us, this creative nature is awakened and excited within us. Words fall from our pen to the page. Notes resonate from the strings of our guitar. Our fingers mold what is impossible to dictate. Our body moves in choreography that we had no hope of arranging.

Creativity is simultaneously humbling and exhilarating. It is profound and yet so simple. It leaves us with a feeling of peace, the knowledge that all is well, and at the same time, we are still anxious, wondering what others will think of the masterpiece we have just created. All of this is worship. All of this adds to the fact that God is so much more than we could ever imagine.

Please don't ever believe that *true* worship includes

only certain procedures—sitting, standing, raising your hands, singing, etc. Worship includes these responses and yet is so much more at the same time. True worship is *creative*, and every aspect of life is hidden in its folds.

Selah Moments

Worship is connecting with God.

❖

Only by His breath can we breathe.
Only by His heartbeat can we survive.

❖

The Holy Spirit hovering over our lives reveals the deep things of God. Deep within God is where creativity begins.

❖

God loves creativity; it is the essence of who He is.

❖

Worship is *creative*, and every aspect of life is hidden in its folds.

Heaven is moving, living, breathing creativity.

❖

All creative people recognize that some mysterious force greater than themselves has breathed and from that breath, what lies before them has materialized.

DAY SIX

Let him kiss me with the kisses of his mouth —
For your love is better than wine.
Because of the fragrance of your good ointments,
Your name is ointment poured forth;
Therefore the virgins love you.
Draw me away!

— SONG OF SOLOMON 1:2–4 —

Love's Effect on Personal Identity

The deeper, hidden levels of intimacy carry a secret that most people cannot bring themselves to touch, for in the touching, change occurs, and blood is let. These hidden levels of intimacy require that all barriers and every other protective countermeasure be removed and the most sensitive places of the soul be touched. It can be frightening. It can be painful to make this secret, solitary journey. No one can make it with us, and few will understand our embarking on it.

If we want to grow closer to the Lord, it will cost us our identity—not just our name, not just our desires, but *everything* that makes us who we are. This is what holiness does to a human; it purges the temple before taking up residency. So if God is to draw close to us, whatever is not of Him must leave the vicinity, for darkness cannot stand His fire—neither can a soul that is desperate to keep its identity.

I'm not saying here that the desires of our hearts, or the works of our hands, are evil and need to be purged. Not at all. But the truth of the matter is that being in the Lord's presence is an all-consuming experience. It is much like standing in the middle of an active volcano—there is nothing in us that is not touched. Only that which is most like Him remains.

Letting Go of Fear

Just by being with Him, we are asking Him to remove our walls. We are asking Him to align our soul with His. We are asking to become one spirit with Him. We are asking to be made holy, which is to be made like Him.

This process can be very difficult for many reasons, and to make matters worse, one thing in particular actively works to keep us from the end result. The chief barrier that blocks us from *real* intimacy with God, thereby keeping us from completely surrendering our lives to Him, is fear.

Fear is not just the enemy of intimacy; it is the assassin. In the Garden of Eden, when Adam and Eve committed the first sin in human history, they hid themselves because they felt ashamed; they were afraid to let God see them.

Because they were responding out of fear, the first thing they did was erect small walls in the form of clothing to keep God at a distance—to keep Him from seeing who they really were. They put up barriers that yelled, "Keep away! We don't know if we can trust You anymore." But obviously, it wasn't God, or His divine nature, who had changed in those few moments.

Fear will lie to us each and every time. It will attempt to convince us that self-protection is more important than being romanced by God and releasing our heart to Him. It will attempt to tell us whatever it can in order to keep us from letting go. But we shouldn't be afraid of God. His intent is not to kill us. It is to *have* us.

The Deeper Level of Abiding

Abiding in Christ means we are willing to bring down our barriers and let go of our fears. Jesus' sacrifice made us perfect forever—this means that there is no condemnation—but being made holy (Christ-like) is a process (Hebrews 10:14). All of us make mistakes, and contrary to what our emotions often tell us, God doesn't expect us to not make them. The truth of the matter is that this romance with Him, filled with grace, rests on *His* shoulders, not ours. So there is nothing to fear.

Because we are so prone to fear, many Christians are content only to abide in Christ, when there is a deeper level of intimacy where *He* abides in *us*. At this level, He is at rest and can make His bed in our heart. Not many of His children actually experience this level of intimacy because we, like Adam and Eve, are loathe to let Him closer. We are afraid that if He sees what we are ashamed of, He will no longer love us—after all, there are so many times we do not love ourselves. So we are afraid. In the touching, change occurs, and blood is let.

Two Become One Flesh

In this romance with God, identity is lost because of a simple but extreme, age-old yet never fully understood principle: True love is much, much more than the glue that holds a couple together. It literally transforms one entity out of two—the two become one flesh. We are lost in the flood of all God is and all He does and all He waits to do. When God becomes all in all in our lives, nothing remains except the gems He Himself has produced in us; the chaff of the world is burned away. In the aftermath, we are left loving God the way we were created to love Him.

Thus we willingly, with great longing, throw off the cloak of ego that hides our true self in order to be clothed in His light, to become one with the fire of His passion. We let Him change us. We let Him uncover our pain. We let Him do these things because we are desperate for Him, because nothing else will satisfy.

Selah Moments

"Let Him kiss me with the kisses
of His mouth, for His love is
better than wine."

❖

How do we respond to the touch
of the Lover?

❖

Just by being with Him, we are asking
Him to remove our walls. We are
asking Him to align our soul with His.
We are asking to be made holy, which
is to be made like Him.

Is there anything we are hiding from Him? Even though we know He already knows about it, denying it is a whole other matter.

❖

Fear is not just the enemy of intimacy; it is the assassin.

❖

True love is much, much more than the glue that holds a couple together. It literally transforms one entity out of two—the two become one flesh.

❖

If we want to grow closer to the Lord, it will cost us our identity. What would it take for us to embark on this journey of the heart?

Day Seven

O God, You are my God;
Early will I seek You;
My soul thirsts for You;
My flesh longs for You
In a dry and thirsty land
Where there is no water.
So I have looked for You in the sanctuary,
To see Your power and Your glory.

— PSALM 63:1–2 —

WORSHIP: AN INSTINCT

*E*ach one of us has supernatural, deep, internal instincts and motivations that are *driving* us toward the Holy One. These urges are God-given, and each time we fail to respond to the prompting of His Spirit, we become a little less whole, a little less alive—a little less human.

Worship is an instinct. It is more than just a happening. It is more than a decision we make at a given time or something we know we *should* do, should we ever find the time to do it. It is an instinct deeply entrenched in our being; we were created to worship *something*. At any given moment, if we are not worshipping God—if we are not living a life that is connected with His—we are worshipping something else. It all goes back to Jesus' statement in Matthew 6: "Where your treasure is, there your heart will be also." In other words, what we focus on we make room for, be that God, our problems, our spouse, fear, or anything else.

If we don't have a deep knowledge of God's consuming love, the paragraph above can sound almost horrific. We read it and something instantly closes down inside us. *I'm not that pure*, we might think. *What am I going to do?*

Most of us are very aware of our faults and shortcomings. Often, those can be the only things we see when we look at ourselves. But this pressure instantly lifts when we realize that God is easy to please. He isn't looking for sacrifice for the sake of sacrifice. If we really want to show Him how much we love Him, then we just show Him. We can tell Him in whatever way comes from our heart. A rose on our desk has the potential to say as much as anything else. A short journal entry can say more than a book of sonnets or an entire day spent on our knees. God has simple tastes. He wants our heart... and that's all.

The Response of the Heart

Therefore, when we stand before Him—the God who, with His own fingers, fashioned everything in existence, the One who calls thunders and lightnings into being and holds the sun still in the sky—when we suddenly find ourselves the end target of His focused gaze, worship can be our only response. It is a response of the heart.

We are driven to this moment. We are driven to see Him as He is. Not all of us will have throne room experiences like the apostle John did, but all of us will have the opportunity to touch the Father's heart on a daily basis. If we consistently miss the subtle urges of His Spirit, we feel it. We might not be able to explain what we feel, but the longer we hold Him off, the more we sense that something is missing. Slowly, life becomes just a series of events that leaves us wondering if this is all there is.

We are driven to worship; that is how He made

us, and we exist on a subhuman level until our heart is in His hands. St. Augustine wrote that we cannot rest until we rest in His presence. How true we have discovered that to be!

Take the Risk

No one can blithely hand us this depth of intimacy with God. Though it is not easy to do, we have to find it ourselves—we have to take a risk with our own heart and not base our relationship with God on the opinions and experiences of others.

We have to dare to change our habits, our lifestyle, our future, our work, our desires, our friends, whatever is necessary—in order to touch what is humanly impossible to touch. To some, this might sound harsh, but as was already stated, touching God really is no different than falling in love. True love, deep love, changes *everything* in order to hold onto and become one with that other person.

This is the greatest challenge, and hence the greatest adventure, we could ever know. We are *driven* to take part in it. Worship—the art of touching

God—is our life breath, our reason, and our purpose beyond all else.

The Outcome of Intimacy

We humans were created with a need to communicate and express ourselves. When we enter the presence of God, we enter a mystical world, an eternal world full of sound and emotion. Here we come face-to-face with the great desire to engage the Divine with what He has given us, with what He has put in our heart. The outgrowth of this experience is that we also want to engage the world with that same drive. The power of God is unstoppable in a Christian who knows the Lover of his or her soul.

To try to touch something we have never touched before is always an experiment—it can be dangerous, and it can be frightening. Yet we live with these supernatural, God-given urges—the deep, internal instincts that continually drive us toward the Holy. I believe we need to take the risk of the unknown. We need to touch the edge of eternity to respond to God with deeper worship. Again, this doesn't require that we all have a "throne room experience." It is our touching, and the being touched by, the Eternal that emboldens us.

When we are where God wants us to be, He will move Heaven and earth to get us to the next place He wants us to be. Even now, when I quiet myself and close my eyes, I can see the throne room. I can feel His living light course through me. I am still blinded by the presence of His glory. And when I open my eyes, I feel just a little out of place...

Selah Moments

The power of God is unstoppable in a Christian who knows the Lover of his or her soul.

❖

True love, deep love, changes everything in order to hold onto and become one with that other person.

❖

Our wholeness depends on our closeness with the Creator.

❖

Worship is not an option; it is an instinct—we *will* worship something. It may be ourselves or some darker force, but we will worship something.

*R*isk the unknown—dare to engage the living God.

❖

*G*od will move Heaven and earth to get us to the next level of intimacy with Him.

About the Author

John Paul Jackson is a husband, father, and established authority on Christian spirituality and dream interpretation. His Biblical approach to dreams reveals their life-changing purpose, and restores an overlooked way God chooses to communicate with people.

John Paul's teachings have stirred and renewed passion for God among people of all ages from various faith backgrounds. His thoughtful "explanations of the unexplainable" and simple, yet profound, concepts help people relate to God and each other in fresh ways.

As an author, speaker, and television guest, John Paul has impacted hundreds of thousands of people, emphasizing character as a key element in the true spiritual life. His many years of study and experience have made him a respected and sought-after spiritual advisor to leaders and believers around the world.

John Paul has shared his practical and spiritual expertise with an International audience through the Streams Training Center courses and publications.

Mystery of Movement

What would it be like to stand before the throne of God?

You would never be the same again! Learn about the interaction of motion, sound, light, color, and energy in Heaven.

1 CD

To order, call 1.888.441.8080
or visit www.streamsministries.com